IS FOR
ALEXANDER

A Historic
Alphabet

by History Unboxed

A NOTE FOR EDUCATORS:

This book includes photographs of historical artwork, including nudity. Additionally, the ancient world was often a violent place. Please preview content.

ALPHA

is for

Alexander

amazing and great

Alexander the Great is one of the most famous conquerors in history. In the 4th century BC/BCE, his empire stretched from Europe to Africa and Asia. He crossed mountains, seas, and deserts. He led an army of tens of thousands of people.

B

BETA

is for

Bucephalus

beloved horse

Bucephalus was a horse no one could tame. Alexander turned the horse towards the sun so Bucephalus could no longer see his own shadow. Once calmed, Bucephalus obeyed Alexander. Alexander rode Bucephalus into many battles.

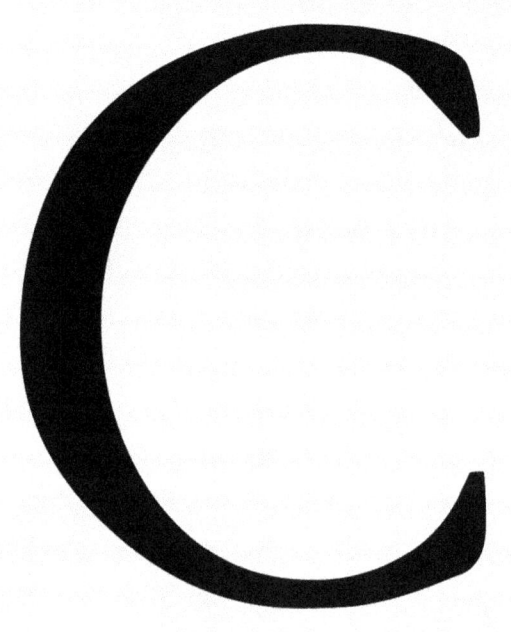

C

is for

Companion

constant and true

Hephaestion was Alexander's closest companion. The two men grew up together and loved each other deeply. When Hephaestion died, Alexander held a lavish funeral and decreed public mourning.

DELTA

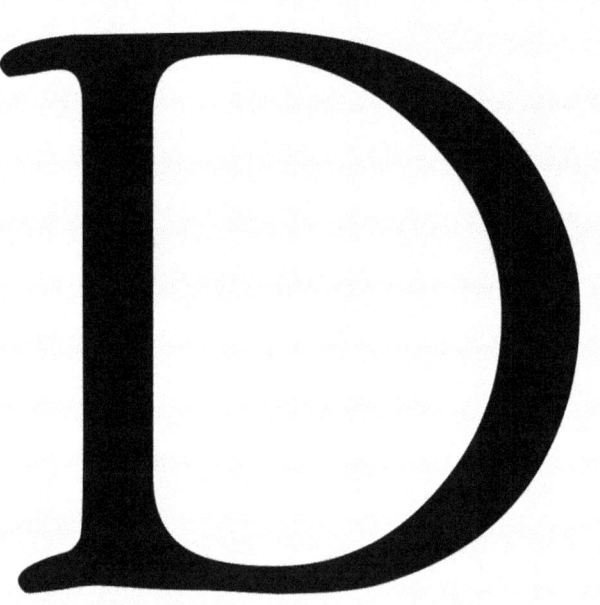

is for

Darius

defeated once and for all

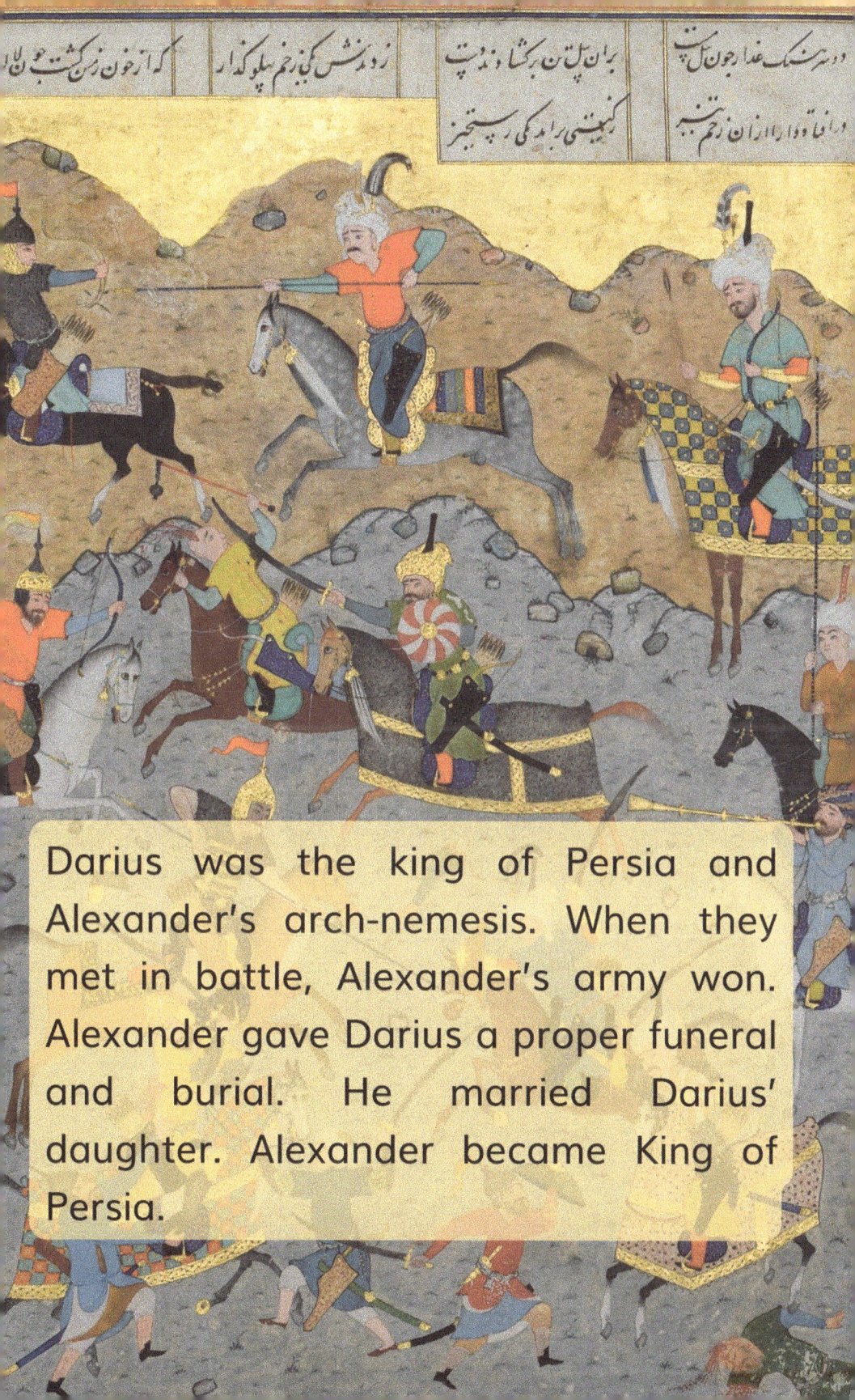

دو ہر سنگ غذا جون لل کشت
بران بل تن برکشا و دپت
زودنش کے زخم پلوکذار
کہینی ربا مدکی رسپتخیز
کر از خون زرکشت جب لا
ورانا وداراان زخم تبہ

Darius was the king of Persia and Alexander's arch-nemesis. When they met in battle, Alexander's army won. Alexander gave Darius a proper funeral and burial. He married Darius' daughter. Alexander became King of Persia.

EPSILON

ETA

is for

Egypt

exceedingly ancient

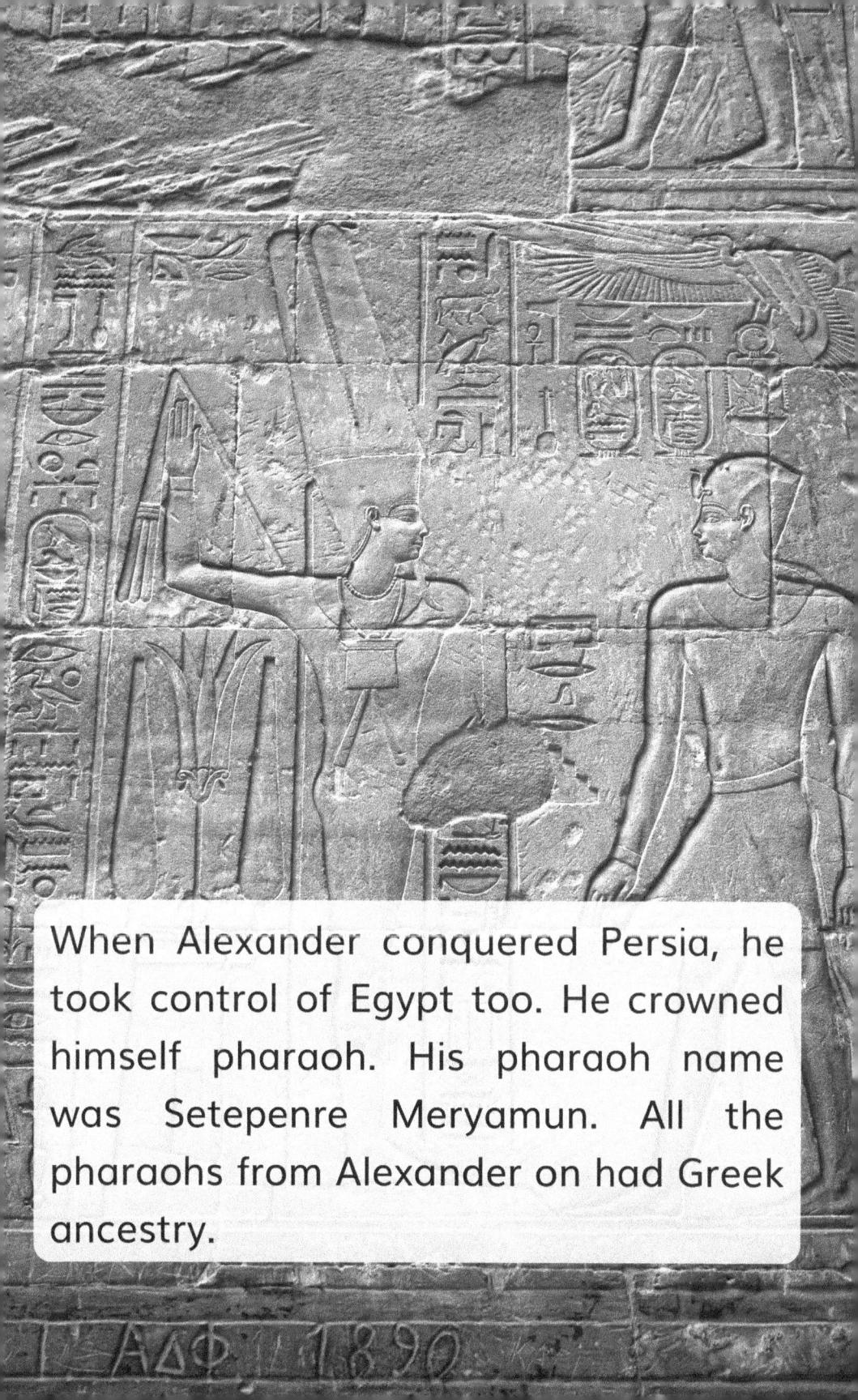

When Alexander conquered Persia, he took control of Egypt too. He crowned himself pharaoh. His pharaoh name was Setepenre Meryamun. All the pharaohs from Alexander on had Greek ancestry.

PHI

is for

Founding

famous cities

Alexander founded around twenty towns. He named many of them after himself. They had names like Alexandroupolis and Alexandria. His cities stretched all the way to western India. This is Alexandria in Egypt.

Γ

GAMMA

G

is for

Gordian Knot

gnarled puzzle to solve

Before the days of Alexander, am oracle predicted that the man who could unravel this knot would become the king of Asia. When Alexander marched on the city of Gordium, he wanted to fulfill the prophecy. He couldn't untie it, so he cut it in half with his sword. From there, he traveled east and conquered most of the parts of Asia known to the ancient Greeks.

H

is for

Honey

holding him in death

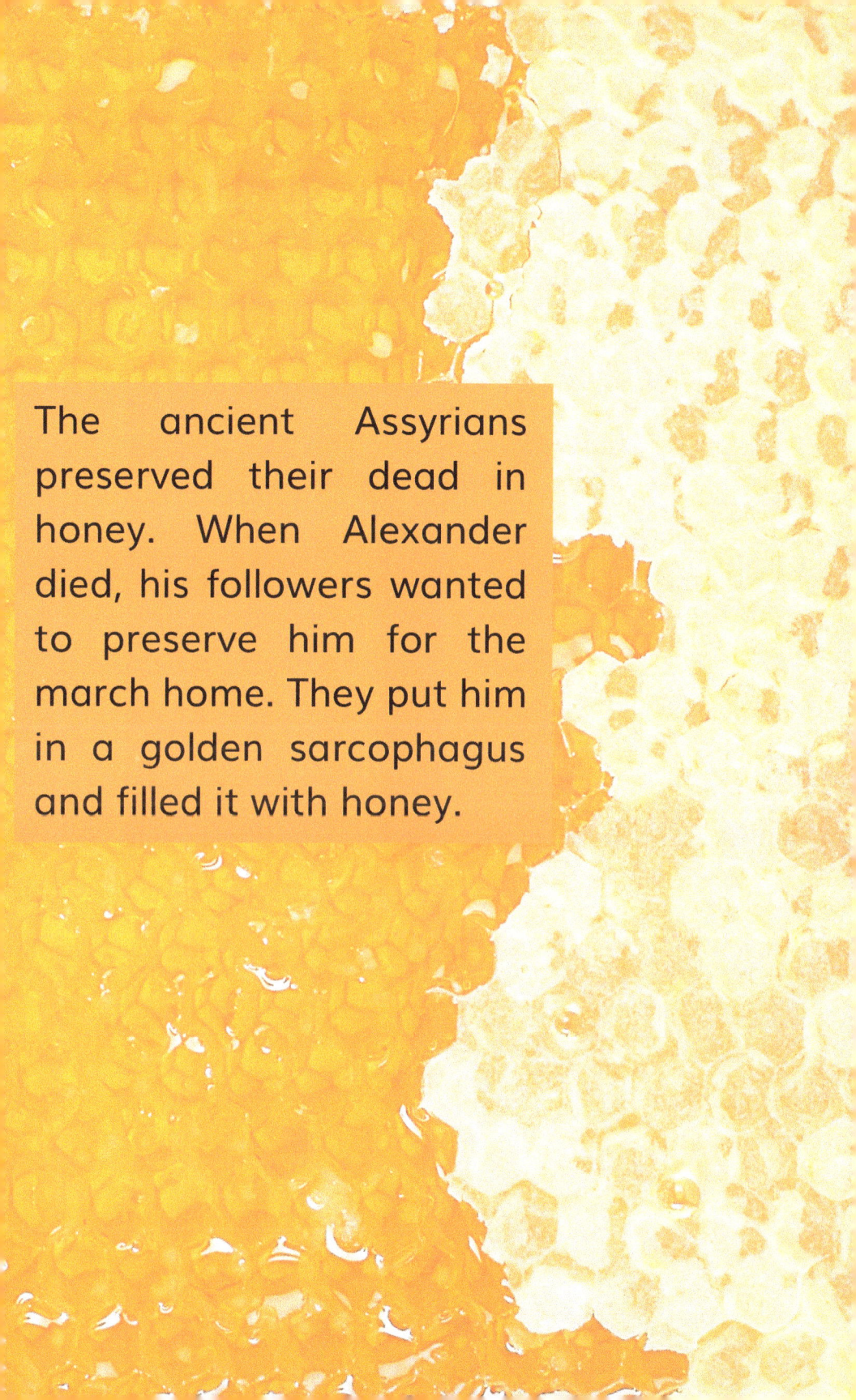

The ancient Assyrians preserved their dead in honey. When Alexander died, his followers wanted to preserve him for the march home. They put him in a golden sarcophagus and filled it with honey.

I

I

is for

India

itinerary's end

Alexander wanted to conquer all of India. But Alexander's army did not want to keep fighting. Alexander's men were homesick. Without their support, Alexander had to turn around.

Beas River in India

J

is for

July

joyful month of his birth

Alexander was born on the sixth day of the month called Hekatombaion. Today, it aligns with July or August.

KAPPA

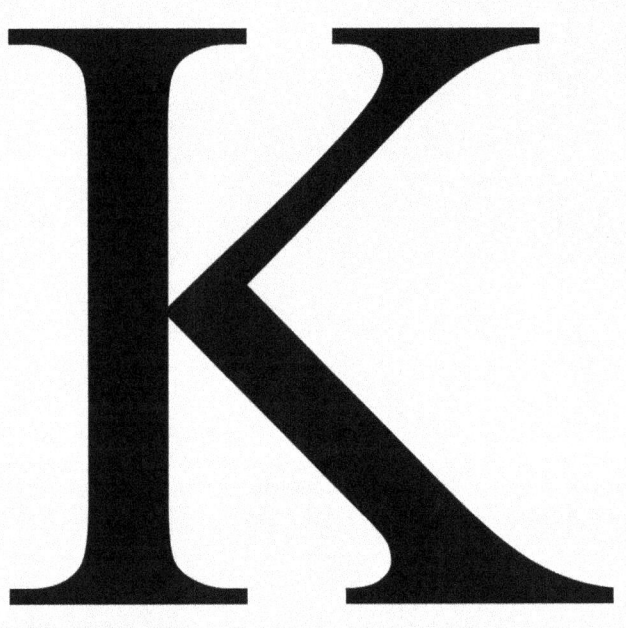

is for

King

kingdom secured

When King Philip died, Alexander acted quickly to take power from other men who had claim to the throne. Alexander became King in 336 BC/BCE. He took other titles as he conquered new lands. He became the King of Persia in 330 BC/BCE.

LAMBDA

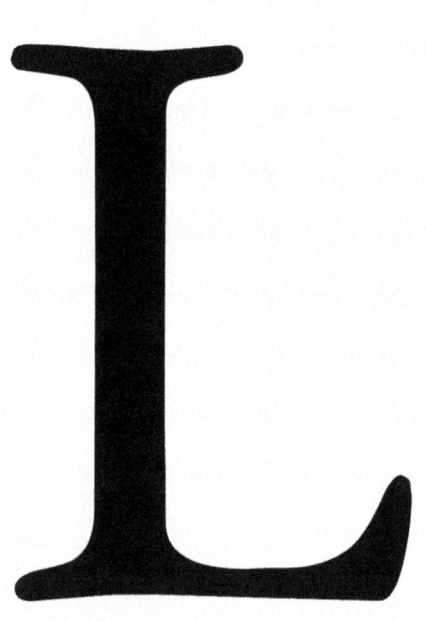

is for

League of Corinth

led by the king

When Philip was king, the Greek kingdoms needed to work together to fight the Persian army. All the city-states except Sparta united under Philip's leadership. The city-states swore oaths to keep peace with each other and follow Philip. Alexander continued his father's work.

M

M

is for

Macedon

Mediterranean home

The kingdom of Macedon was five hundred years old by the time Alexander was born. Under Alexander, the Macedonian Empire became one of the greatest in the ancient world.

N

is for

Nymphaeum

nymph temple school

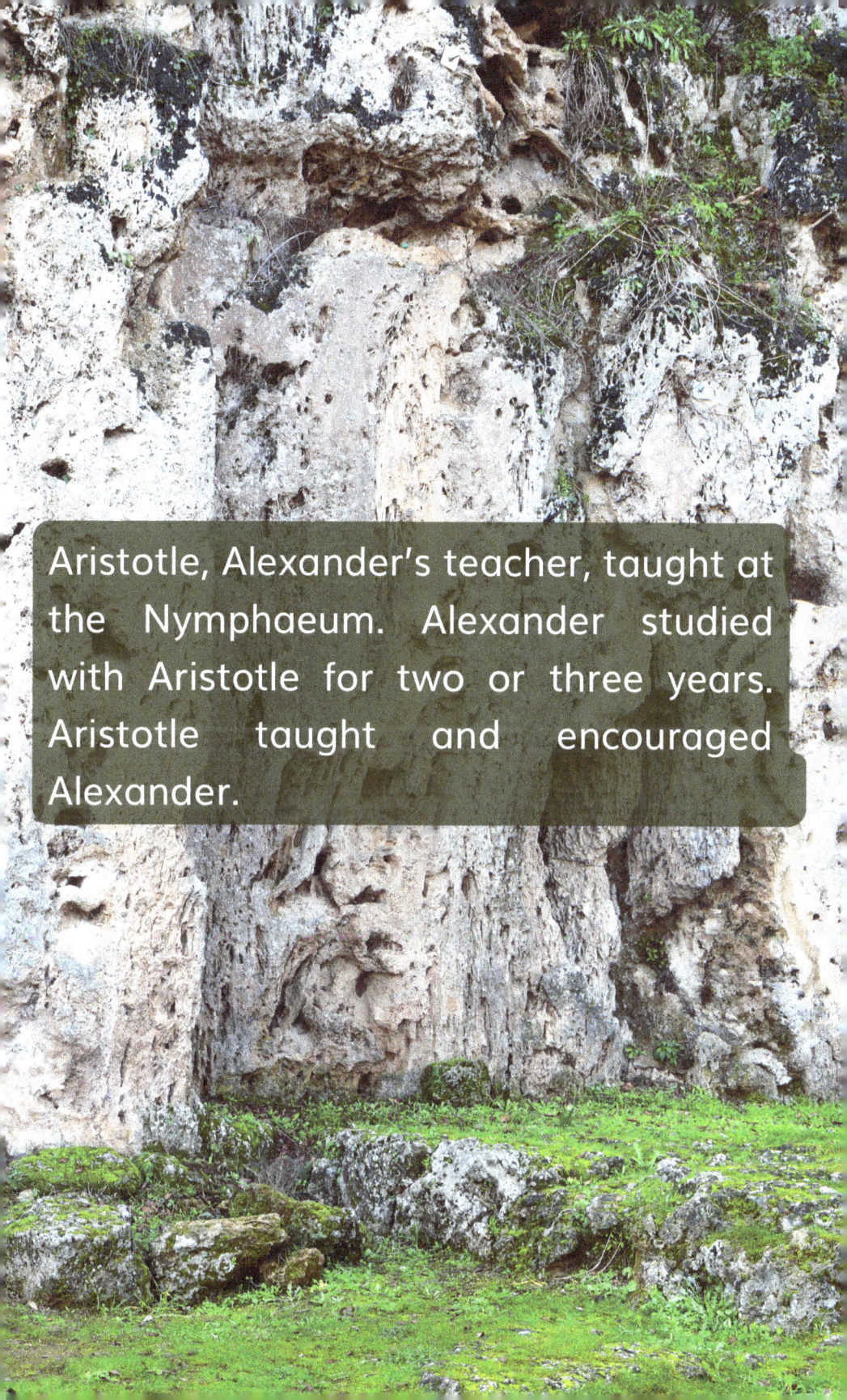

Aristotle, Alexander's teacher, taught at the Nymphaeum. Alexander studied with Aristotle for two or three years. Aristotle taught and encouraged Alexander.

OMEGA
OMIKRON

is for

Olympias

opportunistic mother

Olympias was Alexander's mother. Alexander was not Philip's only son. Olympias would to anything to help Alexander take the throne. Some people believe she poisoned his enemies or had them killed.

Π
PI

P

is for

Philip

proud father

Alexander's father, Philip II of Macedon, ruled for twenty-three years. He turned Macedon from a minor kingdom to the most powerful kingdom in Northern Greece.

is for

Queens

quite a few

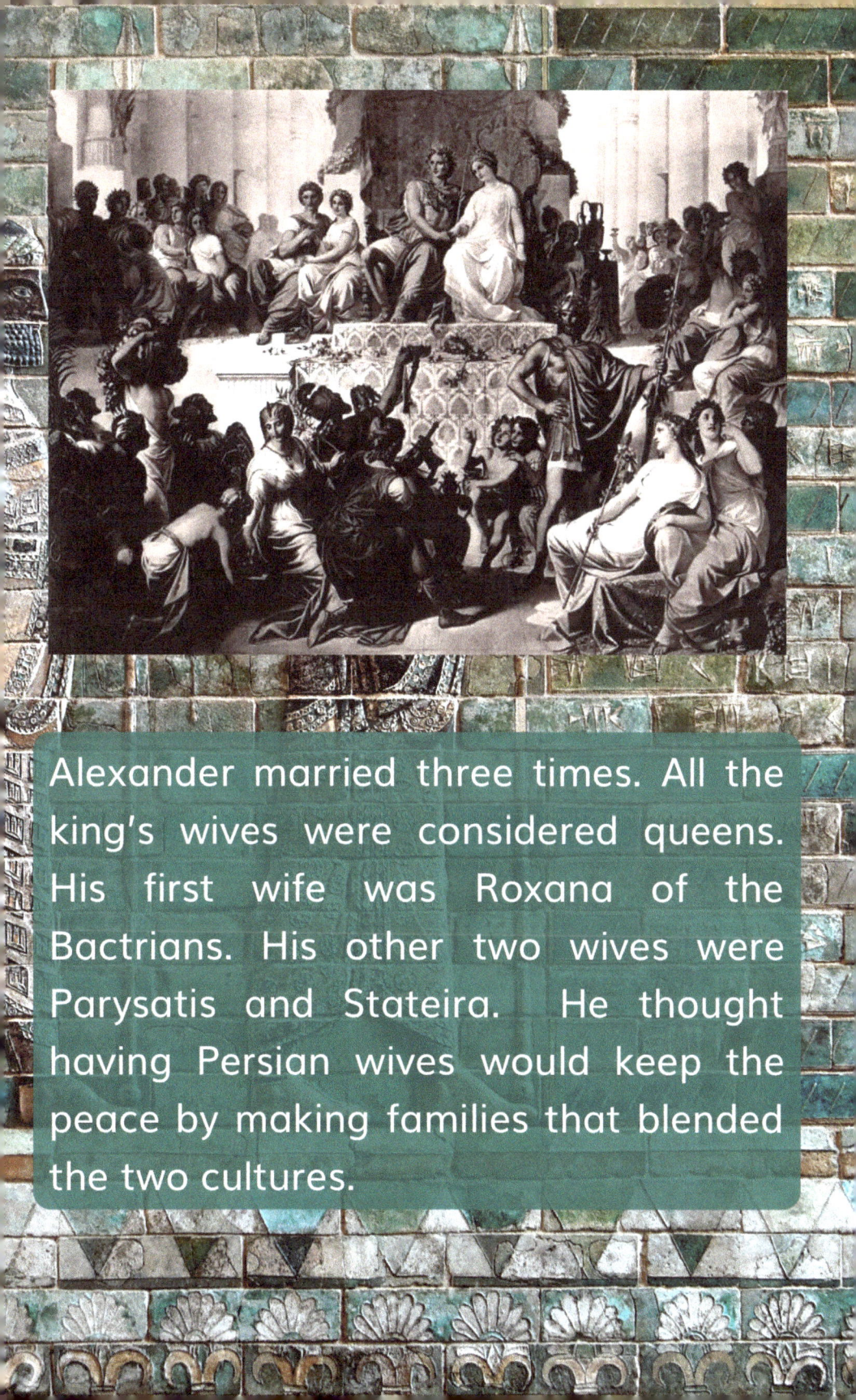

Alexander married three times. All the king's wives were considered queens. His first wife was Roxana of the Bactrians. His other two wives were Parysatis and Stateira. He thought having Persian wives would keep the peace by making families that blended the two cultures.

P
RHO

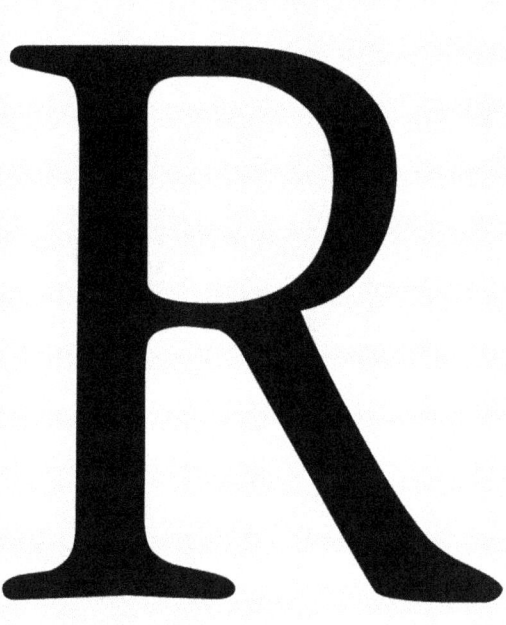

is for

Roxana

royal wife number one

As soon as Alexander saw Roxana, he fell in love with her. Roxana gave birth to Alexander's son a short time after he died. She named the boy after his father.

SIGMA

is for

Stateira

second wife of the king

Stateira was Darius' daughter. It was common practice at the time for conquerors to marry the wife or daughter of the conquered ruler. He also married Stateira's cousin, Parysatis.

T
TAU

is for

Thessalonike

terror of the sea

Thessalonike was Alexander's half-sister. According to legend, she became a mermaid when he died. To each ship she encountered, she asked a question. "Is King Alexander alive?" It was best if the sailors lied to her. If they answered, "He lives and reigns and conquers the world," she let the ship sail away. If they did not, she sank the ship.

Y
UPSILON

is for
Unparalleled
undefeated in war

Alexander the Great started campaigning at sixteen years old. He never lost a campaign in all his years of fighting. He even conquered the great city of Tyre by putting siege engines on ships. No one had ever done that before.

is for

Vast

victorious conquest

The Macedonian Empire under Alexander was the 23rd largest empire in world history. It was larger than the Ottoman Empire, the Roman Empire, and the Byzantine Empire. To the Greeks, it seemed like Alexander had truly conquered the world.

is for

War Elephants

wrecking his plans

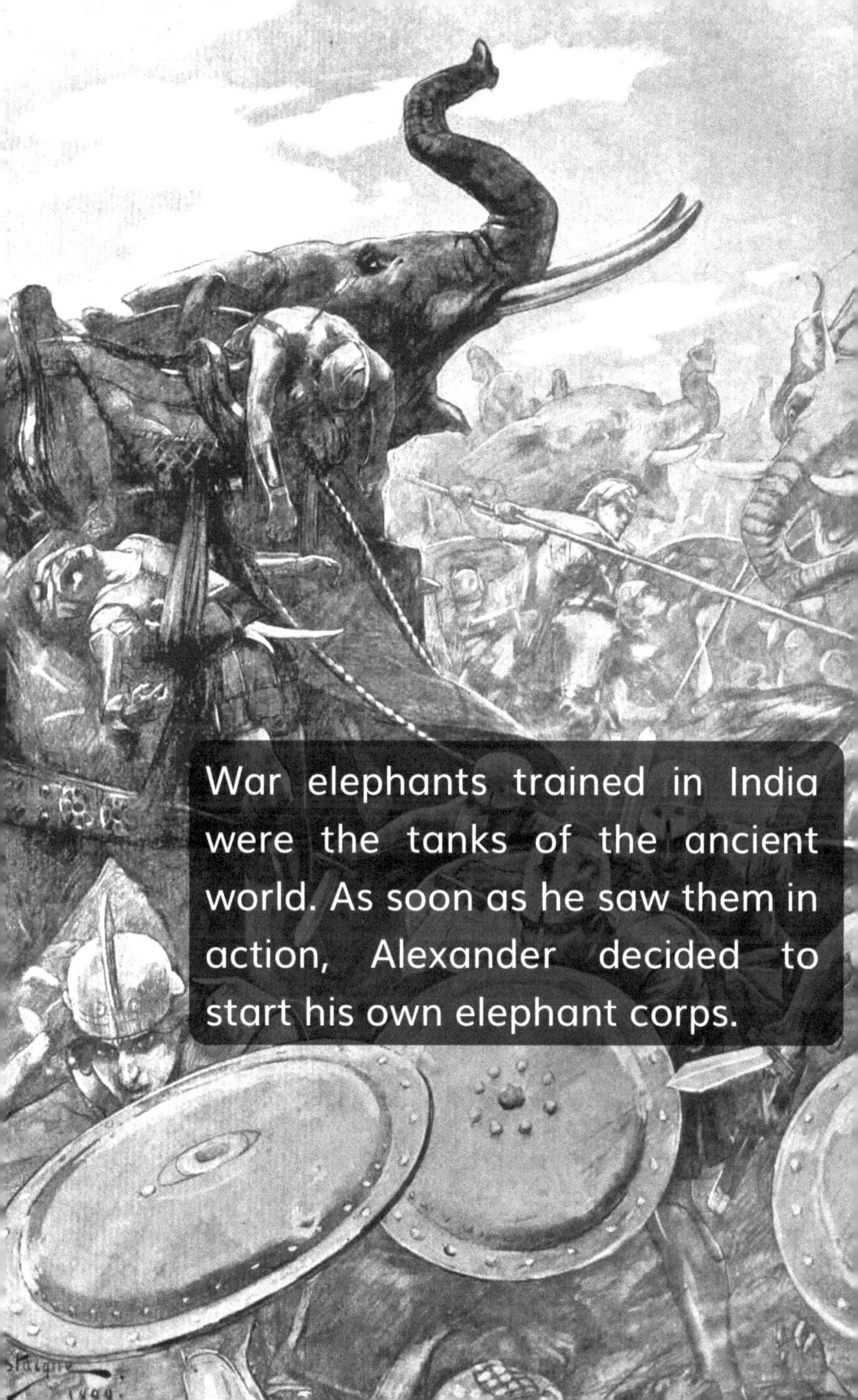

War elephants trained in India were the tanks of the ancient world. As soon as he saw them in action, Alexander decided to start his own elephant corps.

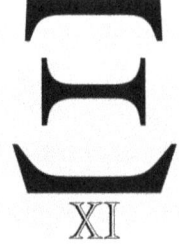

XI

is for

Xerxes

eX king of the Persians

Xerxes the Great was one of the most famous Persian kings. He built a splendid palace in the city of Persepolis. When Alexander conquered Darius, he invaded Persepolis. He burned down Xerxes' once-grand palace.

is for

Youthfulness

young at his death

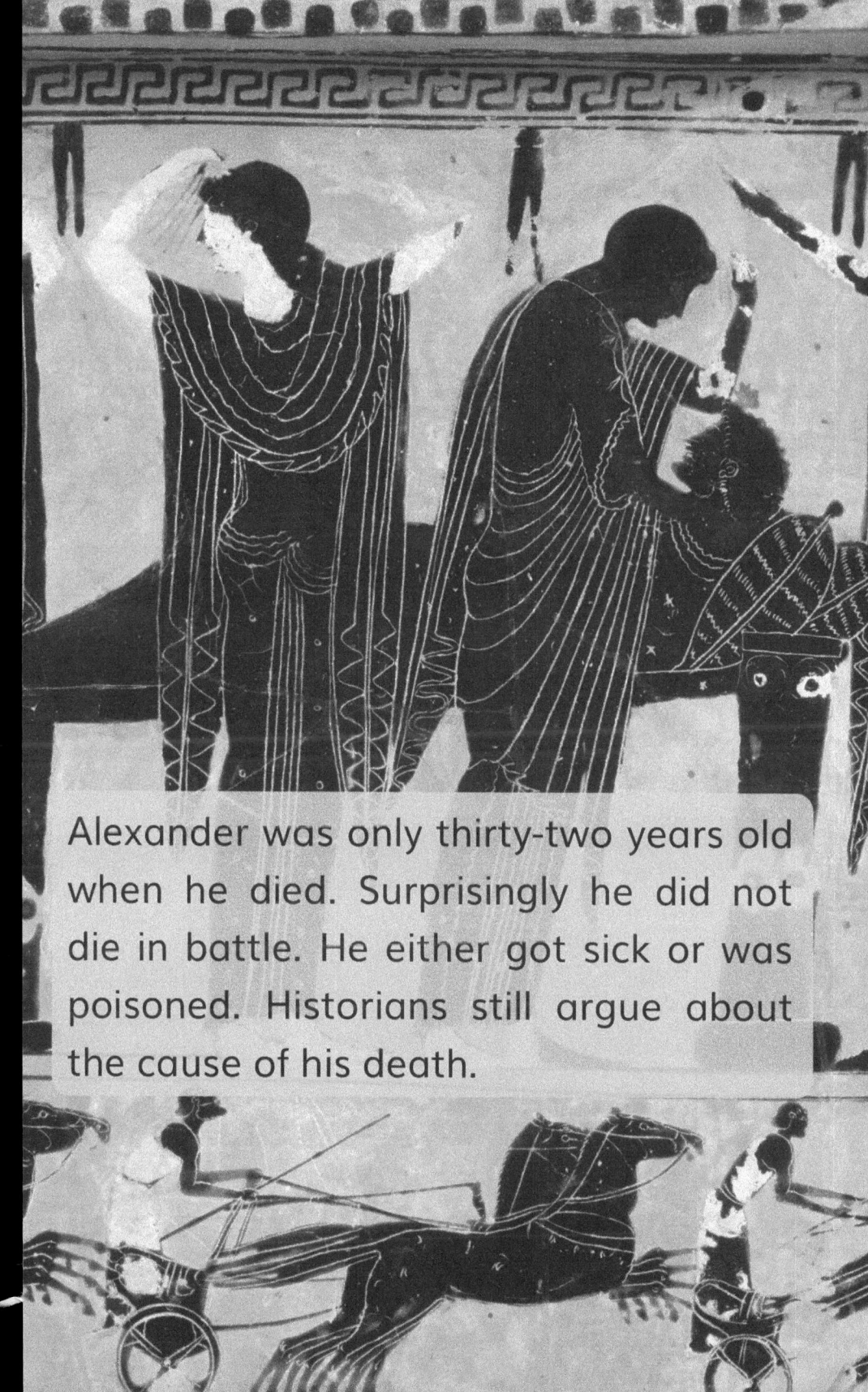

Alexander was only thirty-two years old when he died. Surprisingly he did not die in battle. He either got sick or was poisoned. Historians still argue about the cause of his death.

Z
ZETA

is for

Zoroastrianism

Zaruthustra's religion

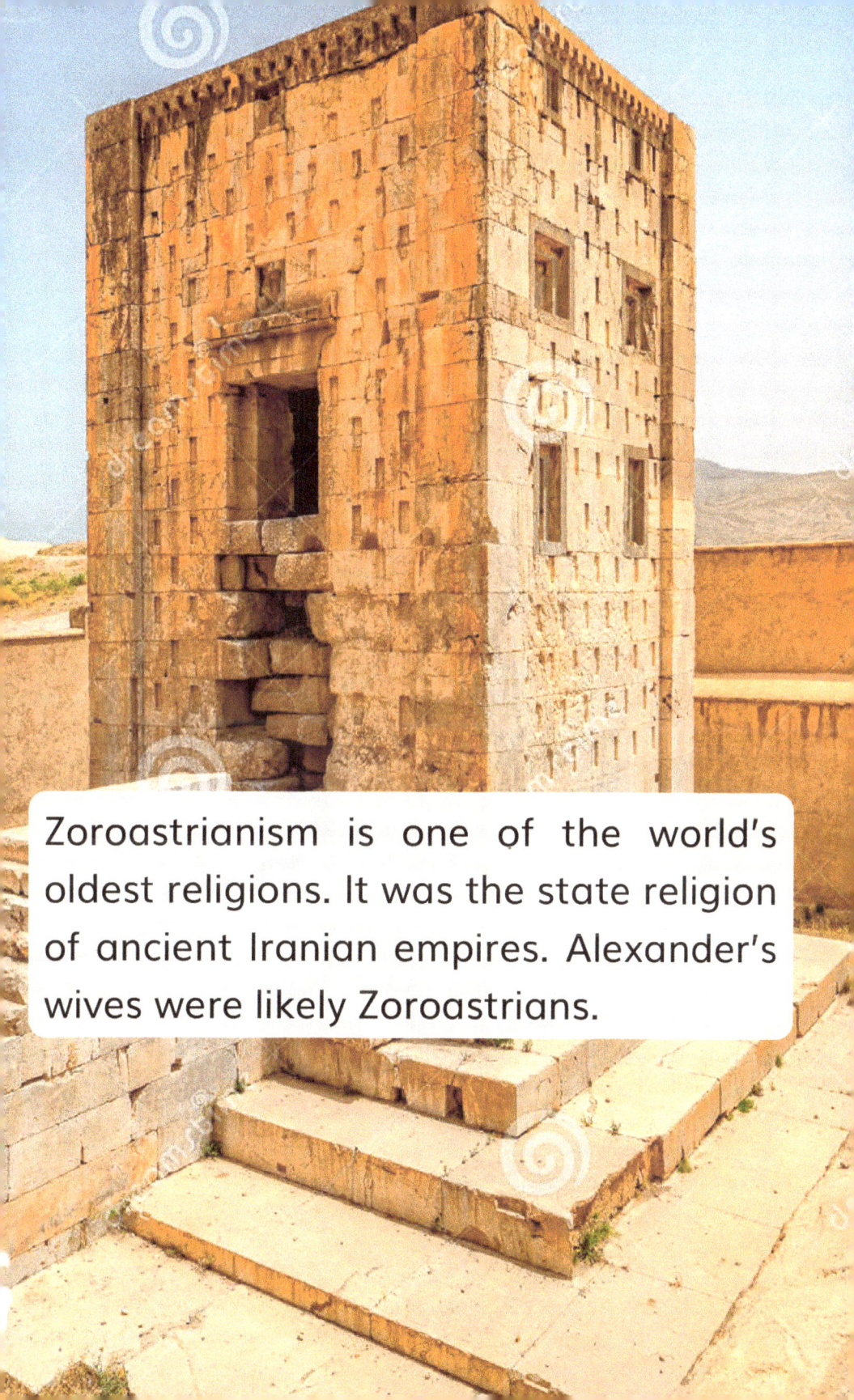

Zoroastrianism is one of the world's oldest religions. It was the state religion of ancient Iranian empires. Alexander's wives were likely Zoroastrians.

ALPHABET NOTES

Letter Name	Greek Capital	Greek Lower-case	English Equivalent
Alpha	A	α	a
Beta	B	β	b
Gamma	Γ	γ	g, n
Delta	Δ		d
Epsilon	E		e
Zeta	Z	ζ	z
Eta	H	η	e
Theta	Θ	θ	th
Iota	I	ι	i
Kappa	K	κ	k
Lambda	Λ	λ	l
Mu	M	μ	m
Nu	N	ν	n
Xi	Ξ	ξ	x
Omicron	O	ο	o
Pi	Π		p
Rho	P	ρ	r
Sigma	Σ	σ OR ς	s
Tau	T	τ	t
Upsilon	Υ	υ	u, y
Phi	Φ	φ	ph
Chi	X	χ	ch
Psi	Ψ	ψ	ps
Omega	Ω	ω	ō

Our modern English alphabet has Mediterranean roots. The Phoenicians adopted their alphabet from Egyptian hieroglyphs. The Greeks traded with the Phoenicians. They started using the same alphabet. They added vowels to make it easier to read. Then the Romans started using Greek letters. By the fall of the Roman Empire, the letters had changed enough to look almost like our upper-case alphabet today. It was still missing J, U, and W. They are the youngest letters. They weren't added until the Middle Ages. Today, people use Greek letters to name fraternities and sororities. Mathematicians and scientists use Greek letters too. The modern Greek alphabet is similar but not identical to Ancient Greek.

Historic Notes

Alexander's origin story has elements of fantasy. His father, King Philip, was said to be descended from Heracles (Hercules), while Alexander's mother, Olympias, claimed to be a descendant of the great hero Achilles. Perhaps it is no wonder that Alexander slept with a copy of the Iliad (the epic poem by Homer which starred Achilles) under his pillow while on his Asian campaign.

Alexander believed that he was destined for greatness, both because of his mythical ancestry and because of predictions from the Oracle at Delphi. Although his campaign into Asia began as a vendetta against the Persians, he had greater plans from the beginning. Always desiring eternal fame, he had historians, poets, sculptors, painters, and musicians accompany his army in order to both record and glorify his accomplishments.

Even where Alexander did not lead an army, you can still find the touch of his influence. He met with ambassadors from the African kingdoms of Cyrene and Ethiopia, from Carthage, and from Italy (perhaps even Rome). Iberian ambassadors came from Spain and Scythians from the Asian steppes. The Celts came from Gaul and Germany. After he died, a fictionalized account of his life called "The Alexander Romance" traveled far and wide. It was one of the most well-known ancient stories.

HISTORY UNBOXED (R)
Book Collection

Ancient History: A Secular Exploration of the World
by Stephanie Hanson and Elizabeth Hauris

Ancient Eats: An Edible Exploration of the World
by Stephanie Hanson

Mysteries of the Rubber People
by Stephanie Hanson

Mysteries of the Shark Hunters (coming in 2023)
by Elizabeth Hauris

C is for Charlemagne
by History Unboxed

The Wizard and the Future King
by Elizabeth Hauris and Stephanie Hanson

To learn more about Alexander the Great and
order hands-on activities, visit
https://www.historyunboxed.com/alexanderabc

www.ingramcontent.com/pod-product-compliance
Lightning Source LLC
Chambersburg PA
CBHW051647120626
46551CB00015B/2252